STEF'S TRUMPET METHOD

*Setup, Maintenance & Development of the Trumpet Embouchure
and an Approach to Jazz Improvisation*

by **STEFFEN KUEHN**

TRUMPOP

PUBLISHING

This Trumpet Method book is dedicated to all the teachers I had the privilege of studying with and all the students that teach me on a daily basis.

Painting by Jeremy Sutton on 2/11/2018 at South Miami-Dade Cultural Arts Center, Cutler Bay, Florida between 8pm–8:30pm on the 2018 'The Art of Jazz' Tour with Tommy Igoe's Birdland All Stars

Front & Back Cover Design: Javier Cabanillas

Illustrations & Layout: Ian Carey

TrumPOP Publishing Logo: Kenya Moses

Back Cover Photo: Lisa Konczal

Editing: Michael Miller & Mary Lekich

Social Media:

facebook.com/steffenkuehnmusic
twitter.com/stef_lof
instagram.com/Steffenkuehn88
youtube.com/TheSteffenKuehn

Contact: info@steffenkuehn.com
Skype Lessons: trumpop_usa

CONTENTS

PREFACE

The purpose of this book is to share my own personal practice routine, which has helped me maintain and develop my trumpet embouchure throughout my career.

The reason being is that the biggest challenge I have encountered in my professional career as a trumpeter has been consistency and endurance.

I have been developing this routine over the last decade and I practice it on a daily basis.

The order of the exercises has been compiled methodically and systematically in one book for maximum benefit.

As a freelancer, I work in many different musical environments. This may range from very strenuous Latin, Rock and Big Band gigs to a mellow Jazz trio or an easier studio recording date. This puts varying degrees of stress on the embouchure and lips, e.g., some nights my lips might be more swollen or I may be substantially more exhausted.

In other words, the demands that are being put on one's embouchure may greatly fluctuate.

That means that my warm-up and my routine should be flexible in order to adjust to those demands, yet it should be consistent in its approach.

I adjust my practice routine based on my physical needs. For instance, after a physically taxing concert I may spend more time on the 'Long Tones Warm-Up' (specifically the 'Pedal Tones') and 'Lip Slurs No.1' or if I feel fresh and relaxed, I choose to practice more of the technically challenging exercises.

This routine requires a commitment for at least a few months in order for your embouchure to develop and respond to the new work-outs.

Hopefully, you will find several helpful techniques that you can then adopt when developing your *own* routine.

The first section, **Anatomy & Physics**, is theoretical and will deal with setup, embouchure, the biology of breathing and the physics of lip vibration and sound production.

The second part, **Warm-Up**, is practical and starts with a solid long tone warm-up (approx. 20 minutes), lip flexibilities and airflow exercises (approx. 15 minutes).

The third part, **Chordal Exercises, Scale Exercises, & Jazz Patterns** goes into chordal and scale exercises/patterns and can be directly applied to your Jazz Improvisation vocabulary.

The fourth part, **Jazz Etudes**, includes Solos over Jazz Standards chord progressions, using material from the previous chapters.

SECTION I: ANATOMY & PHYSICS

Setup & Embouchure

Say the letter 'M' and keep your upper & lower lip slightly pressed on top of each other with the lower lip rolled out a little bit (you will want to see a bit of the red of your lower lip).

Tighten the corners of your mouth slightly.

Keep your chin pointed downwards.

Now take a straw and hold it with your lips/embouchure (not with your teeth) parallel to the ground.

Breathe in through your nose, then push out the air and exhale through the straw while holding the straw with your lips.

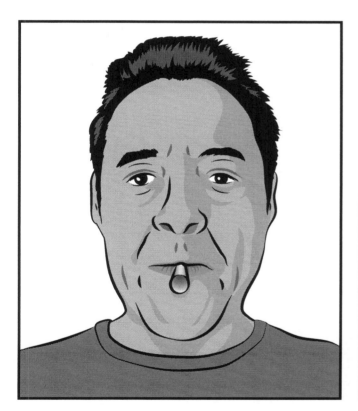

Front View

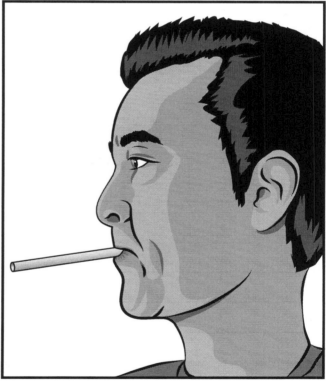

Side View

This is also a very good exercise to strengthen your corners while doing something unrelated, like watching TV, doing homework etc.

Next, take out the straw but keep that same setting in place while placing your Trumpet mouthpiece on this formation.

I find that a ratio of approximately 40% upper lip and 60% lower lip distribution works generally really well (see image below), but there's no 'perfect' proportion for everybody.

You will find that if your aperture (your lip opening) is too wide, no sound or a very airy sound will occur.

At the same token, if your aperture is too small, the air will not pass through your lips properly, since the air is being 'blocked', thus resulting in a pinched or raspy and harsh sound.

Tighten or relax your corners and experiment a little bit with that, until you find the correct opening and tension that will produce a buzz/vibration of the lips. It is my opinion that the lips will vibrate most efficiently when they line up on top of each other (no overbite or underbite of the jaws).

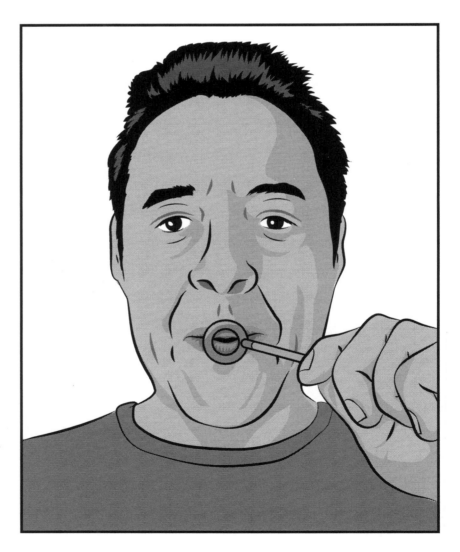

Breathing: Inhale & Exhale

When we breathe in, our Diaphragm flattens out and lowers, thus air is being sucked into our lungs.

Our lungs then inflate sideways, upwards and downwards.

In normal life, this is an unconscious process and we are not really paying attention to any of it.

As Trumpeters (and Wind Instrument players), we depend on air to produce our sounds and notes, so we need to pay good attention to this process!

If we were just to open our mouth without any other physical activity, no air would be expelled!

That's why we are pushing our Diaphragm, abdominal muscles and muscles from our rib cage upwards and from the sides against the lungs, thus pressuring the air out of the lungs, which is how we control the exhalation/speed and compression of our air.

The speed and compression of the exhaled air is dependent on how hard or soft we push from those muscle groups against the lungs.

A very extreme example of very fast expelled air is coughing!

Inhaling

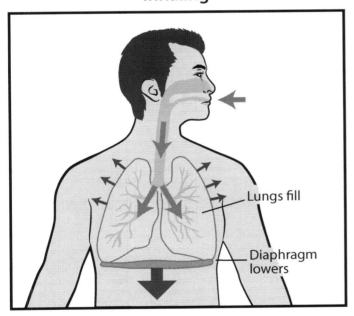

Exhaling

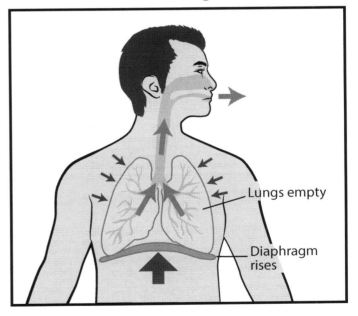

Physics: Lip Vibration & Sound Production

The frequency of the lip vibration is the fundamental frequency of our note, as is the vibration of a reed for Woodwind players, the vibration of a string for String players or the vibration of the vocal cords for Singers—they all share the same concept in Physics, that a higher vibration/frequency will result in a higher pitched note.

So, if we want to play a higher note on the Trumpet, we must increase our airspeed to get the lips to vibrate at a higher rate!

That means, we have to generate higher/faster air compression and speed, which is a function of expelling air from our lungs at a faster rate (as explained in the previous section **Breathing: Inhale & Exhale**).

Air Speed vs. Tongue Position

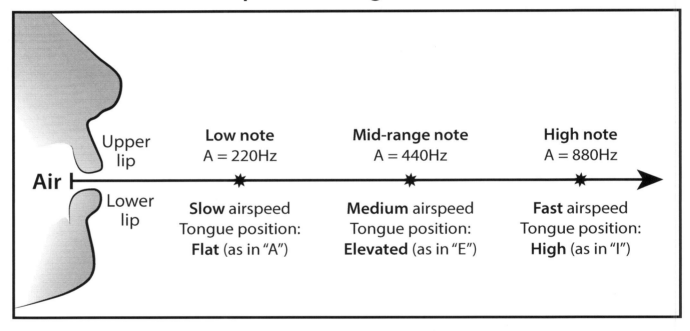

	Low note A = 220Hz	Mid-range note A = 440Hz	High note A = 880Hz
	Slow airspeed Tongue position: **Flat** (as in "A")	**Medium** airspeed Tongue position: **Elevated** (as in "E")	**Fast** airspeed Tongue position: **High** (as in "I")

In addition, for the high and extreme register of the Trumpet, we need to raise the position of the back of our tongue to generate even more airspeed and air compression.

By making the cavity between the roof of the mouth and the raised tongue smaller, we can now add the extra compression to our air column, which in turn will result in a faster vibration of our lips, which in turn will result in a higher note!

Tongue Positions and Related Vowels

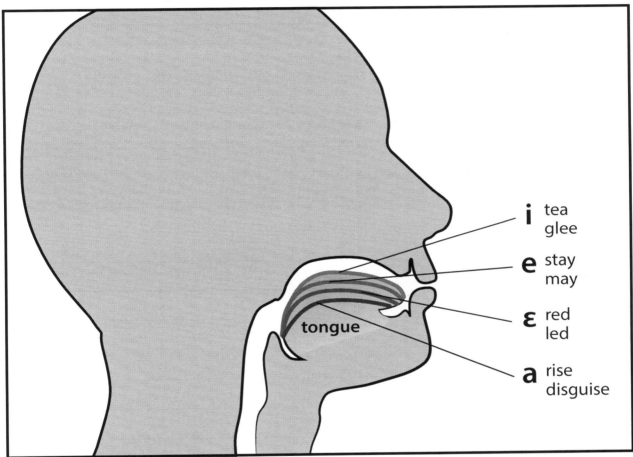

At the same time, we need to tighten the muscles in the corners proportional to the increased air pressure to withstand the faster air column and to hold the embouchure in place (otherwise the lips will roll out and the embouchure collapses).

Long Tones & Pedal Tones

Hold the notes for a full breath, make sure your airstream is steady and that you are playing with a good sound! You can play the notes below 'Pedal C' open if that's easier.

Daily Warm-Up: Long Tones

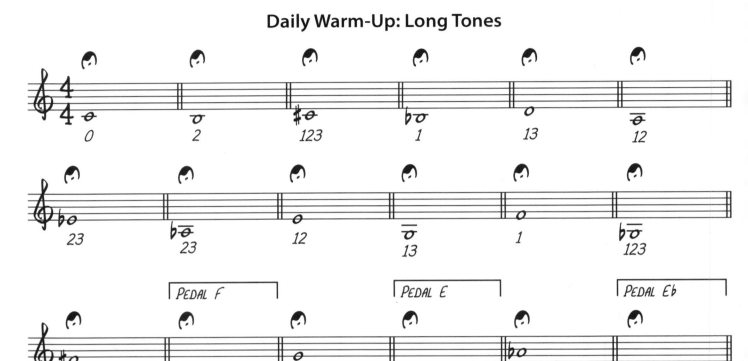

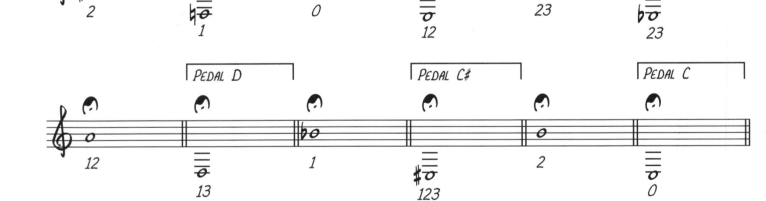

(continued)

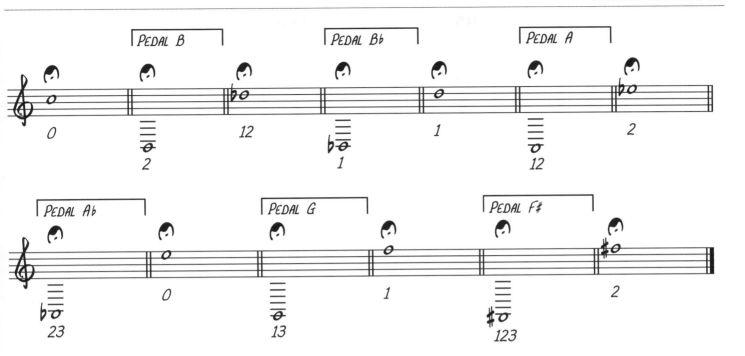

Lip Flexibilities/Airflow Exercise

Play Lip Flexibilities No. 1 – No. 6 slurred and make sure to lock in every partial.

Focus on consistent airflow and the arch of your tongue. For the ascending melodic line, you want to arch your tongue higher in small degrees. For the descending melodic line, you flatten your tongue in small degrees.

Also focus on tightening the muscles in the corners proportional to the increasing air pressure to withstand the faster air column and, vice versa, relaxing the muscles in the corners proportional to the decreased air pressure.

Play as many repetitions as you like, but play at least as many as marked in one breath! You can extend Lip Flexibilities No. 5 by adding partials to the top note, thus using this exercise to slowly and gradually increase your range.

Daily Warm-Up: Lip Flexibilities No. 1

Daily Warm-Up: Lip Flexibilities No. 2

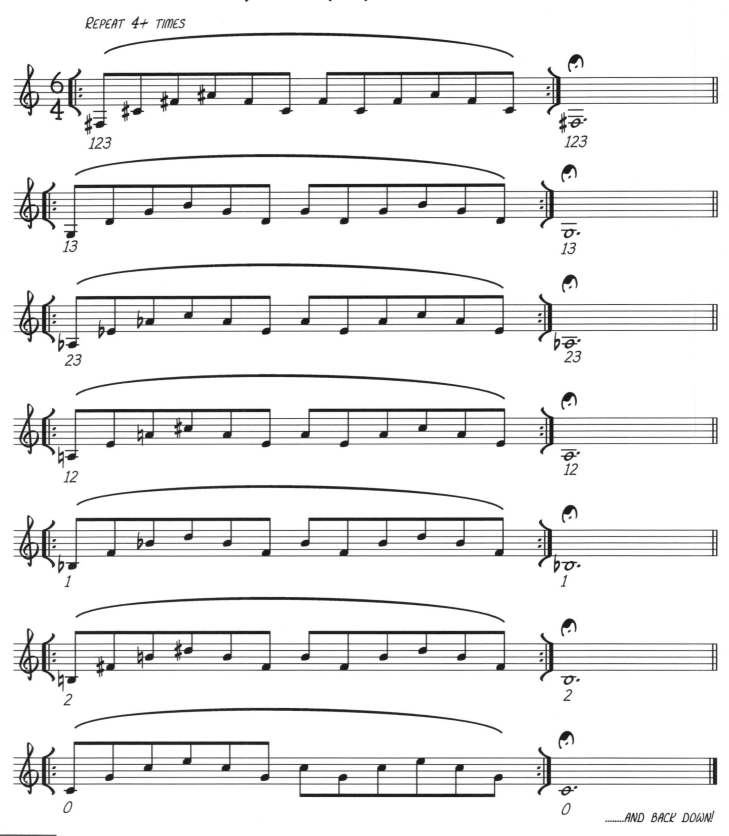

........AND BACK DOWN!

Daily Warm-Up: Lip Flexibilities No. 3

Daily Warm-Up: Lip Flexibilities No. 4

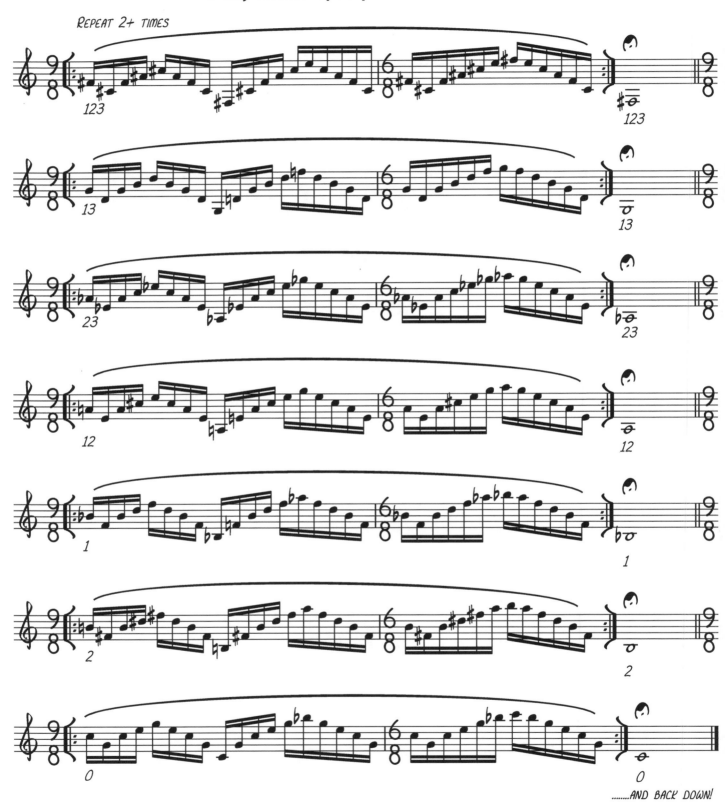

Daily Warm-Up: Lip Flexibilities No. 5

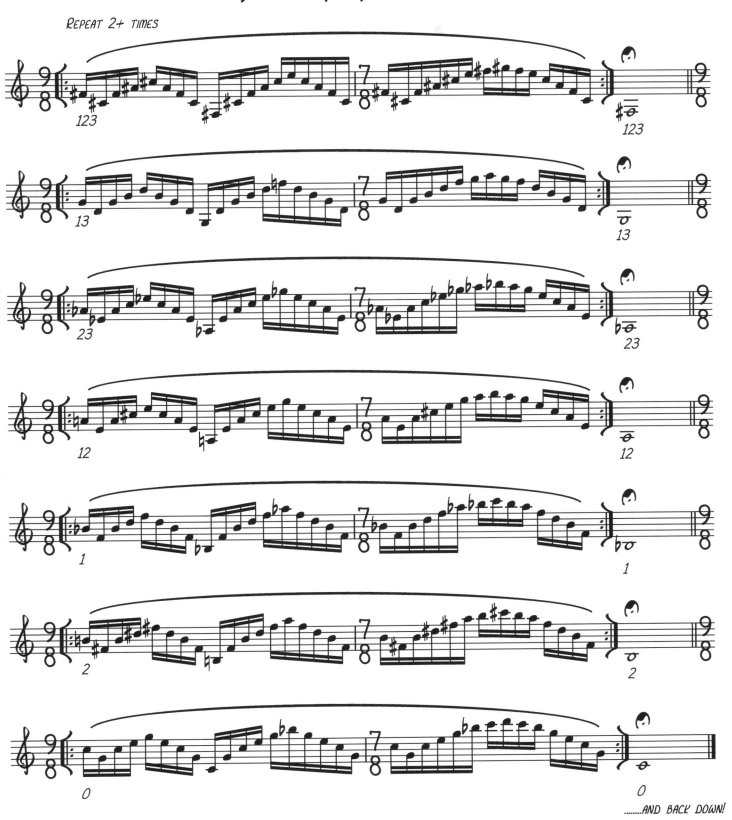

........AND BACK DOWN!

Daily Warm-Up: Lip Flexibilities No. 6

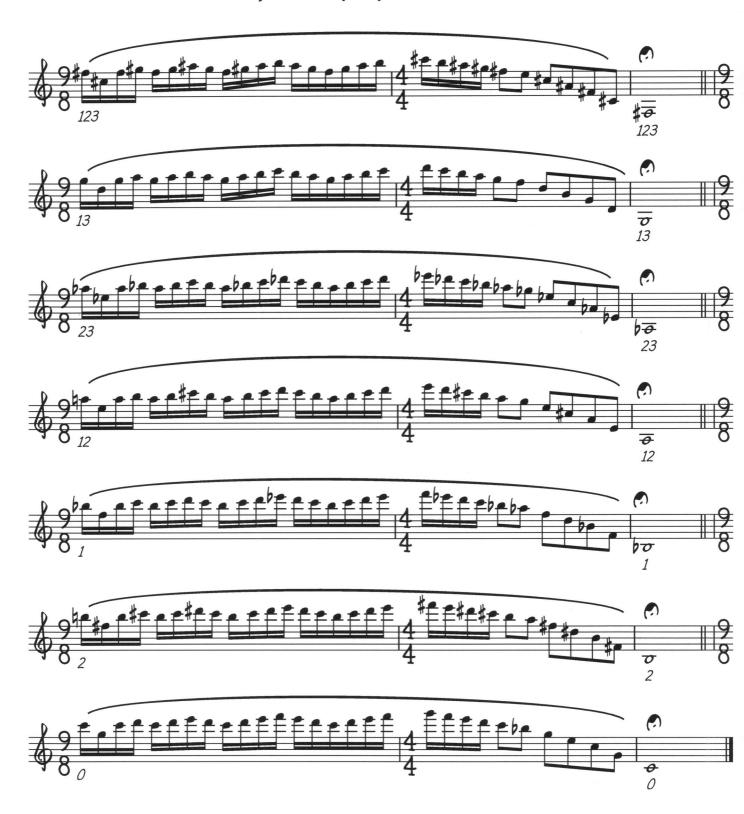

Chromatic Scale/Airflow Exercise

Play all Chromatic Scales slurred and make sure to focus on your consistent airflow while keeping your 'air behind the note'!

You can extend the Chromatic Scale by going up in half steps, thus using this exercise to slowly and gradually increase your range as well.

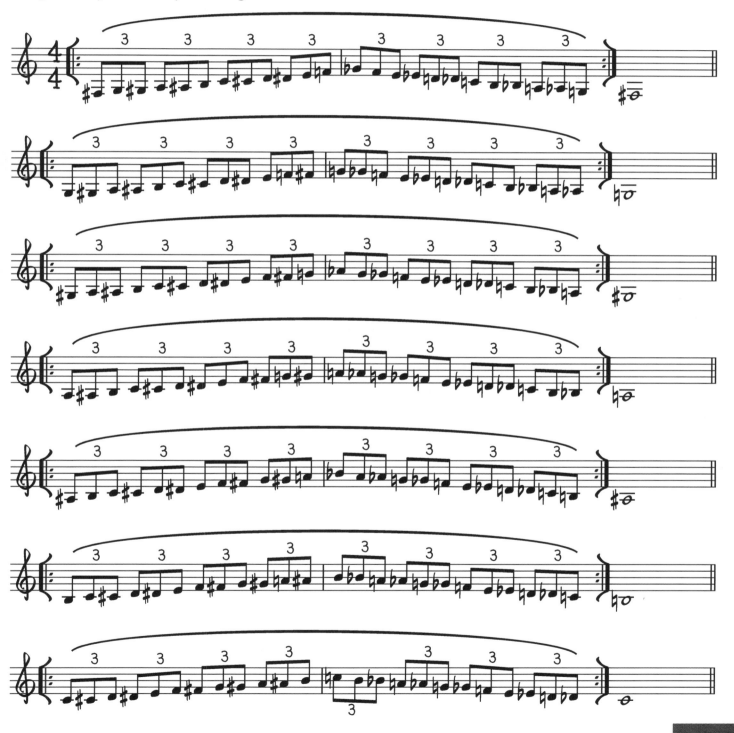

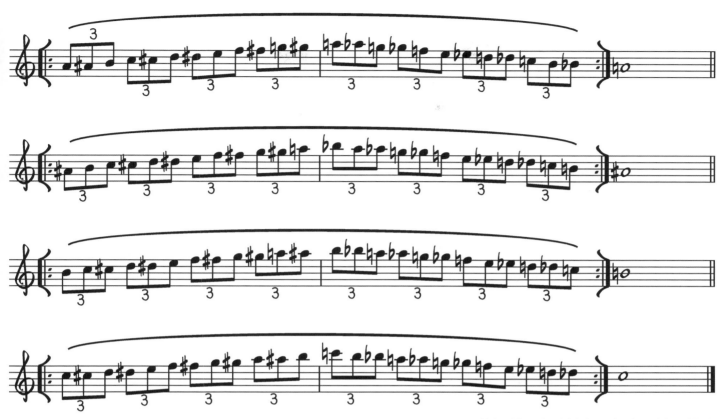

CONTINUE TO PLAY AS HIGH AS YOU PLEASE

SECTION III: AN APPROACH TO JAZZ IMPROVISATION

Chordal Exercises, Scale Exercises & Jazz Patterns

In Section III you will find the Circle of 5ths, the Modes of the Major Scale, Melodic Minor Scale and Harmonic Minor Scale.

On the scale sheets, the small Roman numerals indicate 'Minor' and the capitalized Roman numerals indicate 'Major'.

Now substitute the Roman numeral with the chord letter and you'll find the scale that fits the chord symbol.

It is my opinion that with all the modes of these 3 scale groups, you will cover the majority of all the chord symbols that you will encounter in Jazz Improvisation (there are scales that are not related to these 3 groups, for example the Blues scale, the Whole Tone scale, the Whole-Half Diminished, the Half-Whole Diminished and other more exotic scales).

All exercises in Section III should be articulated!

The first Chordal Exercise presents the 5 Qualities of the 7th Chord:

- Major 7 (Ionian)
- Dominant 7 (Mixolydian)
- Minor 7 (Dorian, Aeolian)
- Half-Diminished 7 (Locrian, 2nd Mode Harmonic Minor)
- Full-Diminished 7 (Whole-Half Diminished)

The second Chordal Exercise presents the diatonic 7th chords in the Major key:

- I Chord up (Ionian)
- ii Chord down (Dorian)
- iii Chord up (Phrygian)
- IV Chord down (Lydian)
- V Chord up (Mixolydian)
- vi Chord down (Aeolian)
- vii Chord up (Locrian)

The third Chordal Exercise presents the diatonic 7th chords in the Melodic Minor key:

- i Chord up (Melodic Minor)
- ii Chord down (Dorian ♭2)
- III Chord up (Lydian Augmented)
- IV Chord down (Lydian Dominant)
- V Chord up (Mixolydian ♭6)
- vi Chord down (Locrian #2)
- vii Chord up (Half-Diminished Chord, but is used mostly as Superlocrian over a V7alt with a Major 3rd—it's a hybrid!)

(Keep in mind that other musicians might use different nomenclature for these scales.)

The fourth Chordal Exercise presents the diatonic 7th chords in the Harmonic Minor key:

- i Chord up (Harmonic Minor)
- ii Chord down (2nd Mode Harmonic Minor)
- III Chord up (3rd Mode Harmonic Minor)
- iv Chord down (4th Mode Harmonic Minor)
- V Chord up (5th Mode Harmonic Minor)
- VI Chord down (6th Mode Harmonic Minor)
- vii Chord up (7th Mode Harmonic Minor)

The Scale Exercise must be articulated and tongued!

I chose the Superlocrian scale, since it has the ♭9, #9, #11 and ♭13 as its alterations and is used frequently over the V7alt Dominant Chord.

Use different scales for this scale exercise, for example the Lydian Dominant, which gives you the #11, or 5th Mode Harmonic Minor, which includes the ♭9 and ♭13 as its altered notes.

Then apply Exercise #1 (1-3-4-2 pattern) to your chosen scale and practice that pattern.

You can then apply different patterns to your chosen scale, like 1-2-3-5, 5-3-2-1 or 1-2-3-1 or make up your own patterns.

The Circle of Fifths

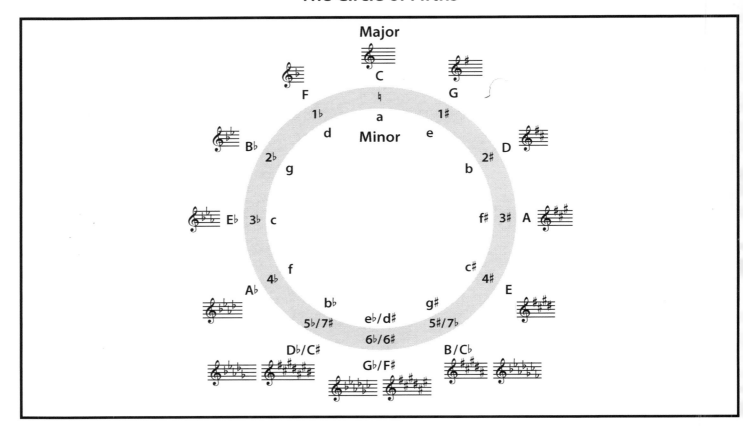

Modes of the Major Scale

Name	Ionian	Dorian	Phrygian	Lydian	Mixolydian	Aeolian	Locrian
Symbol	I Maj7 I △7	ii min7 ii–7	iii min7 iii–7	IV Maj7#11 IV △7#11	V7	vi min7 vi–7	vii–7♭5 vii ∅7
C Major	C	D	E	F	G	A	B
G Major	G	A	B	C	D	E	F#
D Major	D	E	F#	G	A	B	C#
A Major	A	B	C#	D	E	F#	G#
E Major	E	F#	G#	A	B	C#	D#
B Major	B	C#	D#	E	F#	G#	A#
F# Major	F#	G#	A#	B	C#	D#	E#
G♭ Major	G♭	A♭	B♭	C♭	D♭	E♭	F
D♭ Major	D♭	E♭	F	G♭	A♭	B♭	C
A♭ Major	A♭	B♭	C	D♭	E♭	F	G
E♭ Major	E♭	F	G	A♭	B♭	C	D
B♭ Major	B♭	C	D	E♭	F	G	A
F Major	F	G	A	B♭	C	D	E

Modes of the Melodic Minor Scale

Name	Melodic Minor	Dorian ♭2	Lydian Augmented	Lydian Dominant	Mixolydian ♭6	Locrian ♮2	Superlocrian
Symbol	i min♮7 i–♮7	ii min7 ii–7	III Maj7♯5 III △7♯5	IV 7♯11	V 7♭13	vi–7♭5 vi ∅7	VII 7alt*
C Mel. Minor	C	D	E♭	F	G	A	B
G Mel. Minor	G	A	B♭	C	D	E	F♯
D Mel. Minor	D	E	F	G	A	B	C♯
A Mel. Minor	A	B	C	D	E	F♯	G♯
E Mel. Minor	E	F♯	G	A	B	C♯	D♯
B Mel. Minor	B	C♯	D	E	F♯	G♯	A♯
F♯ Mel. Minor	F♯	G♯	A	B	C♯	D♯	E♯
G♭ Mel. Minor	G♭	A♭	B♭♭	C♭	D♭	E♭	F
D♭ Mel. Minor	D♭	E♭	F♭	G♭	A♭	B♭	C
A♭ Mel. Minor	A♭	B♭	C♭	D♭	E♭	F	G
E♭ Mel. Minor	E♭	F	G♭	A♭	B♭	C	D
B♭ Mel. Minor	B♭	C	D♭	E♭	F	G	A
F Mel. Minor	F	G	A♭	B♭	C	D	E

*Superlocrian functions as a V7^{ALT}, even though its chord quality is vii ∅7.

Modes of the Harmonic Minor Scale

Name	1st Mode Har. Minor	2nd Mode Har. Minor	3rd Mode Har. Minor	4th Mode Har. Minor	5th Mode Har. Minor	6th Mode Har. Minor	7th Mode Har. Minor
Symbol	i min♮7 i–♮7	ii –7♭5 ii ∅7	III Maj7♯5 III △7♯5	iv –7	V 7♭9 ♭13	VI Maj7♯11 VI △7♯11	vii dim7 vii o7
C Har. Minor	C	D	E♭	F	G	A♭	B
G Har. Minor	G	A	B♭	C	D	E♭	F♯
D Har. Minor	D	E	F	G	A	B♭	C♯
A Har. Minor	A	B	C	D	E	F	G♯
E Har. Minor	E	F♯	G	A	B	C	D♯
B Har. Minor	B	C♯	D	E	F♯	G	A♯
F♯ Har. Minor	F♯	G♯	A	B	C♯	D	E♯
G♭ Har. Minor	G♭	A♭	B♭♭	C♭	D♭	E♭♭	F
D♭ Har. Minor	D♭	E♭	F♭	G♭	A♭	B♭♭	C
A♭ Har. Minor	A♭	B♭	C♭	D♭	E♭	F♭	G
E♭ Har. Minor	E♭	F	G♭	A♭	B♭	C♭	D
B♭ Har. Minor	B♭	C	D♭	E♭	F	G♭	A
F Har. Minor	F	G	A♭	B♭	C	D♭	E

F#

5 Qualities of the 7th Chord

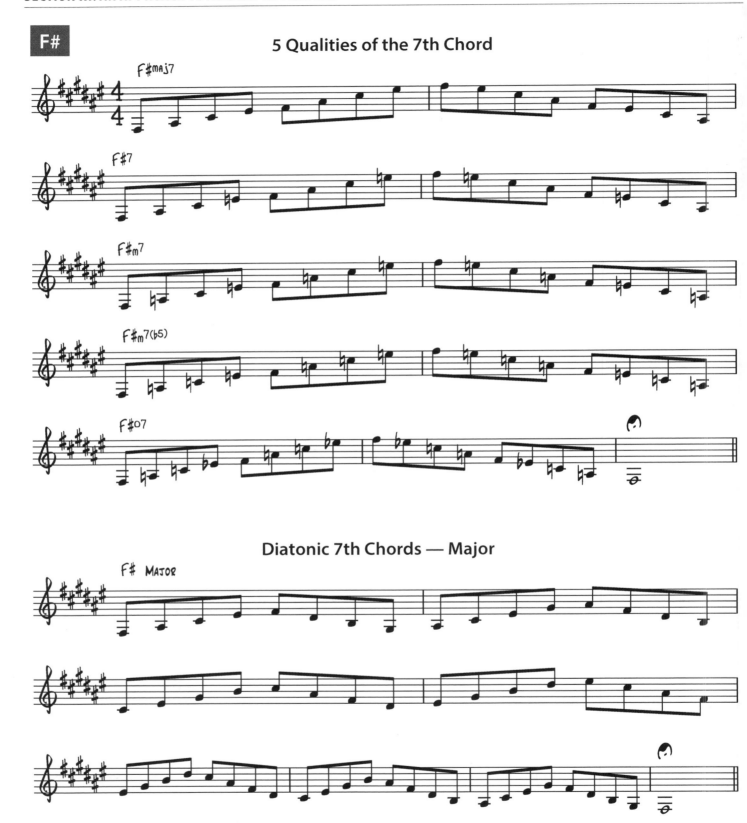

Diatonic 7th Chords — Major

F# *(continued)*

Diatonic 7th Chords — Melodic Minor

Diatonic 7th Chords — Harmonic Minor

F# *(continued)*

Superlocrian — 7th Mode, Melodic Minor

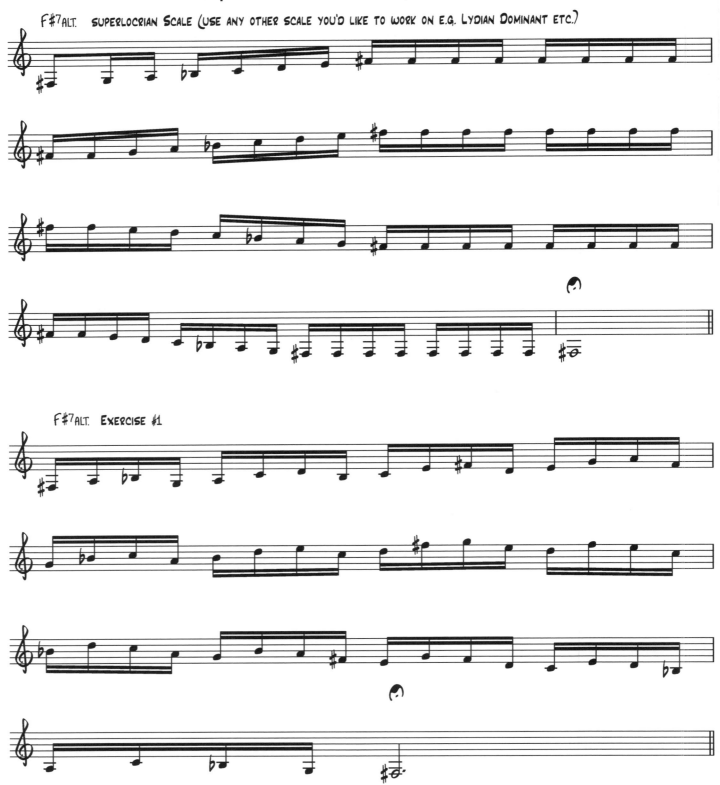

F# *(continued)*

5 Qualities of the 7th Chord

Diatonic 7th Chords—Major

G *(continued)*

Diatonic 7th Chords—Melodic Minor

Diatonic 7th Chords—Harmonic Minor

G *(continued)*

Superlocrian—7th Mode, Melodic Minor

G7alt. Superlocrian Scale (use any other scale you'd like to work on e.g. 5th Mode Harmonic Minor etc.)

G7alt. Exercise #1

G *(continued)*

G⁷ALT. EXERCISE #2

G⁷ALT. EXERCISE #3

G⁷ALT. EXERCISE #4

G⁷ALT. EXERCISE #5

5 Qualities of the 7th Chord

Diatonic 7th Chords—Major

Ab *(continued)*

Diatonic 7th Chords—Melodic Minor

Diatonic 7th Chords—Harmonic Minor

Ab *(continued)*

Superlocrian—7th Mode, Melodic Minor

Ab7 ALT.   SUPERLOCRIAN SCALE (USE ANY OTHER SCALE YOU'D LIKE TO WORK ON E.G. LYDIAN DOMINANT ETC.)

Ab7 ALT. EXERCISE #1

A♭ (continued)

A♭7 ALT. **EXERCISE #2**

A♭7 ALT. **EXERCISE #3**

A♭7 ALT. **EXERCISE #4**

A♭7 ALT. **EXERCISE #5**

A

5 Qualities of the 7th Chord

Diatonic 7th Chords—Major

A *(continued)*

Diatonic 7th Chords—Melodic Minor

Diatonic 7th Chords—Harmonic Minor

A *(continued)*

Superlocrian—7th Mode, Melodic Minor

A7ALT.   SUPERLOCRIAN SCALE (USE ANY OTHER SCALE YOU'D LIKE TO WORK ON E.G. 2ND MODE HARMONIC MINOR ETC.)

A7ALT. EXERCISE #1

A (continued)

A⁷ALT. EXERCISE #2

A⁷ALT. EXERCISE #3

A⁷ALT. EXERCISE #4

A⁷ALT. EXERCISE #5

5 Qualities of the 7th Chord

Diatonic 7th Chords—Major

B♭ *(continued)*

Diatonic 7th Chords—Melodic Minor

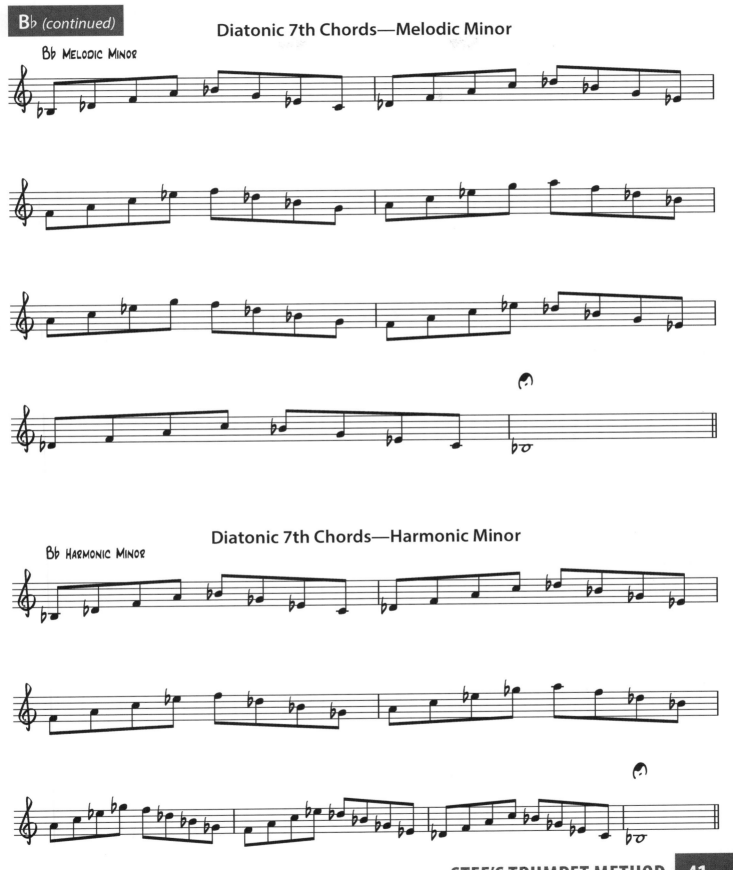

Diatonic 7th Chords—Harmonic Minor

B♭ *(continued)*

Superlocrian—7th Mode, Melodic Minor

B♭7 ALT.   SUPERLOCRIAN SCALE (USE ANY OTHER SCALE YOU'D LIKE TO WORK ON E.G. LOCRIAN ETC.)

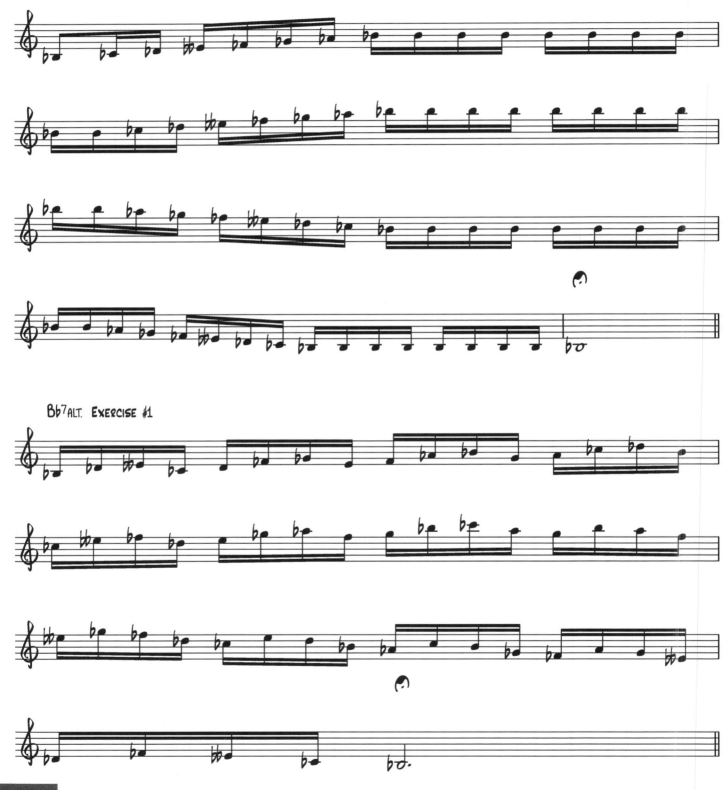

B♭7 ALT. EXERCISE #1

Bb *(continued)*

Bb7ALT. EXERCISE #2

Bb7ALT. EXERCISE #3

Bb7ALT. EXERCISE #4

Bb7ALT. EXERCISE #5

B

5 Qualities of the 7th Chord

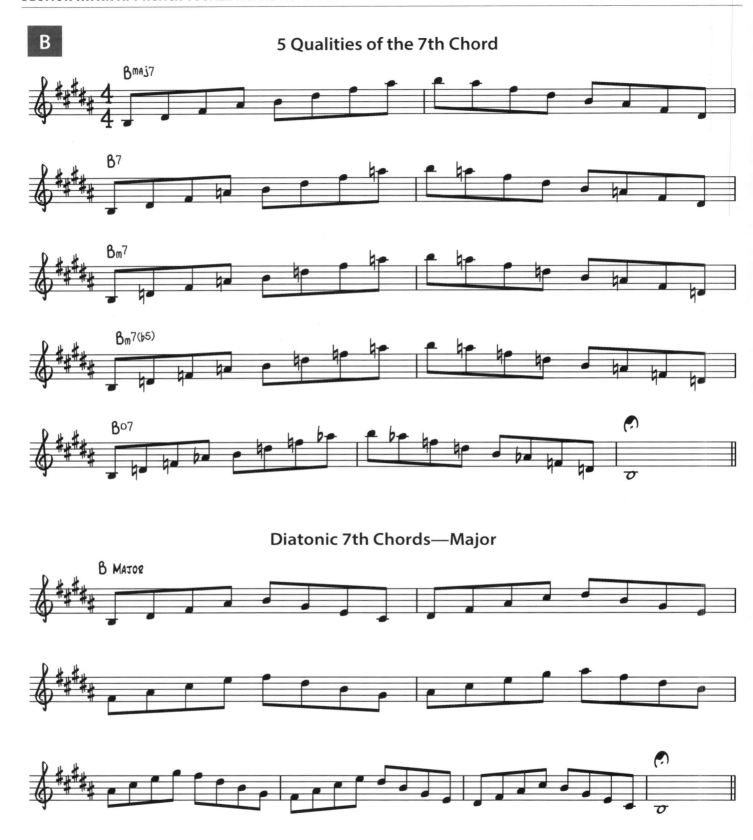

Diatonic 7th Chords—Major

B (continued)

Diatonic 7th Chords—Melodic Minor

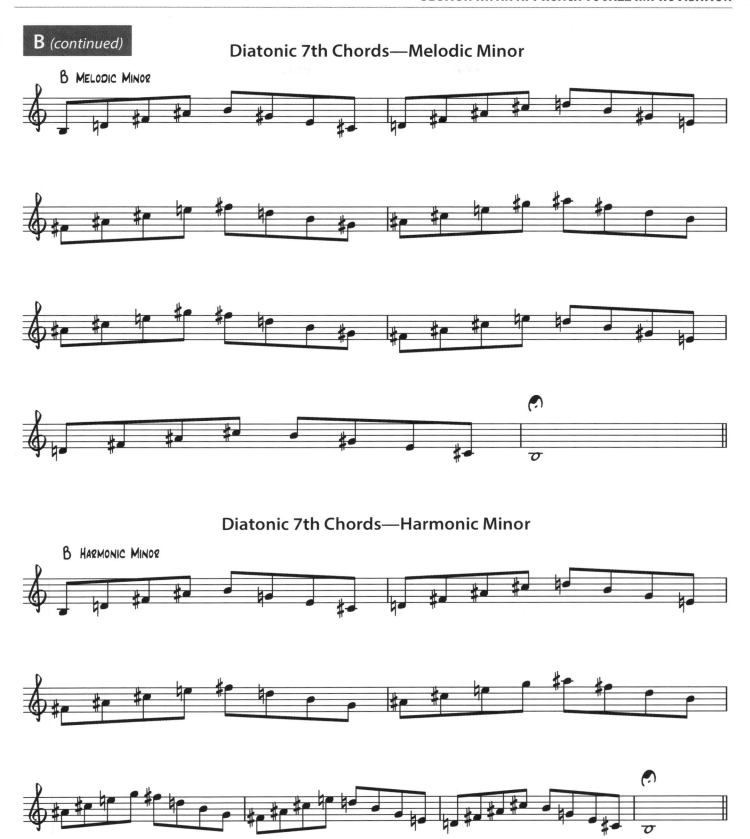

Diatonic 7th Chords—Harmonic Minor

B *(continued)*

Superlocrian—7th Mode, Melodic Minor

B⁷ALT.   SUPERLOCRIAN SCALE (USE ANY OTHER SCALE YOU'D LIKE TO WORK ON E.G. LYDIAN ETC.)

B⁷ALT. EXERCISE #1

B *(continued)*

B7 ALT. EXERCISE #2

B7 ALT. EXERCISE #3

B7 ALT. EXERCISE #4

B7 ALT. EXERCISE #5

C

5 Qualities of the 7th Chord

Diatonic 7th Chords—Major

C (continued)

Diatonic 7th Chords—Melodic Minor

Diatonic 7th Chords—Harmonic Minor

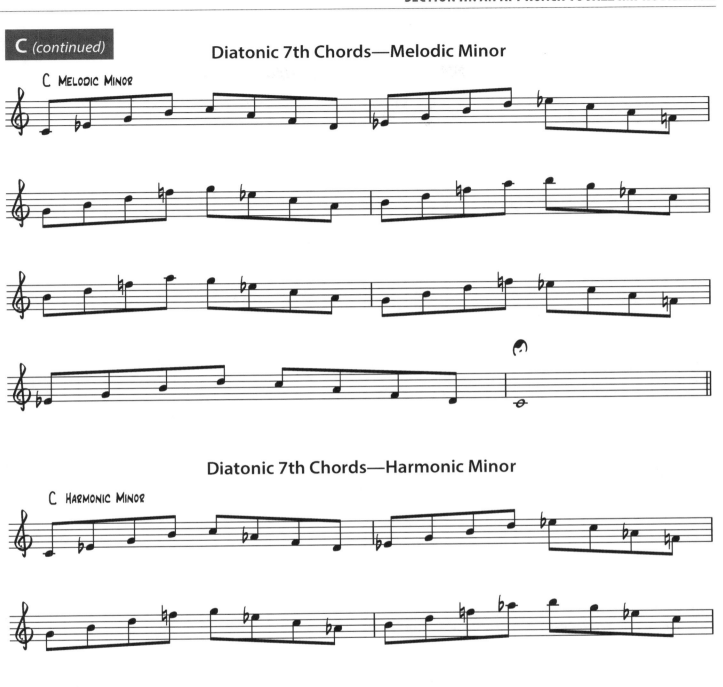

C *(continued)*

Superlocrian—7th Mode, Melodic Minor

C7ALT.   SUPERLOCRIAN SCALE (USE ANY OTHER SCALE YOU'D LIKE TO WORK ON E.G. MIXOLYDIAN ETC.)

C7ALT. EXERCISE #1

C *(continued)*

C7 ALT. EXERCISE #2

C7 ALT. EXERCISE #3

C7 ALT. EXERCISE #4

C7 ALT. EXERCISE #5

Db

5 Qualities of the 7th Chord

Diatonic 7th Chords—Major

Db *(continued)*

Diatonic 7th Chords—Melodic Minor

Db MELODIC MINOR

Diatonic 7th Chords—Harmonic Minor

Db HARMONIC MINOR

Db *(continued)*

Superlocrian—7th Mode, Melodic Minor

Db7ALT. SUPERLOCRIAN SCALE (USE ANY OTHER SCALE YOU'D LIKE TO WORK ON E.G. DORIAN ETC.)

Db7ALT. EXERCISE #1

D♭ *(continued)*

D♭7 ALT. EXERCISE #2

D♭7 ALT. EXERCISE #3

D♭7 ALT. EXERCISE #4

D♭7 ALT. EXERCISE #5

D

5 Qualities of the 7th Chord

Diatonic 7th Chords—Major

D *(continued)*

Diatonic 7th Chords—Melodic Minor

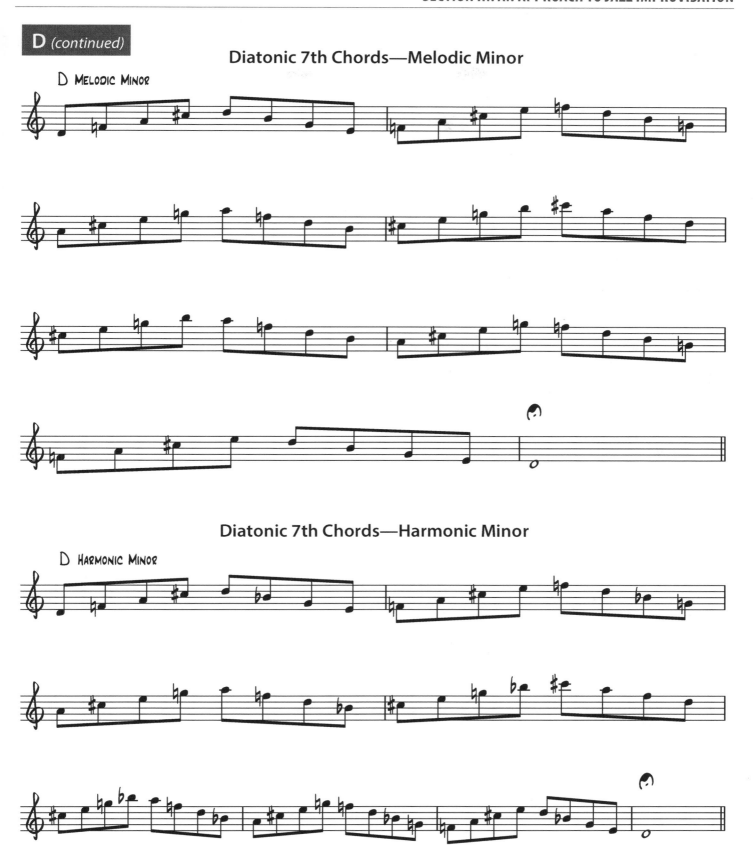

Diatonic 7th Chords—Harmonic Minor

D *(continued)*

Superlocrian—7th Mode, Melodic Minor

D⁷ALT. SUPERLOCRIAN SCALE (USE ANY OTHER SCALE YOU'D LIKE TO WORK ON E.G. LYDIAN DOMINANT ETC.)

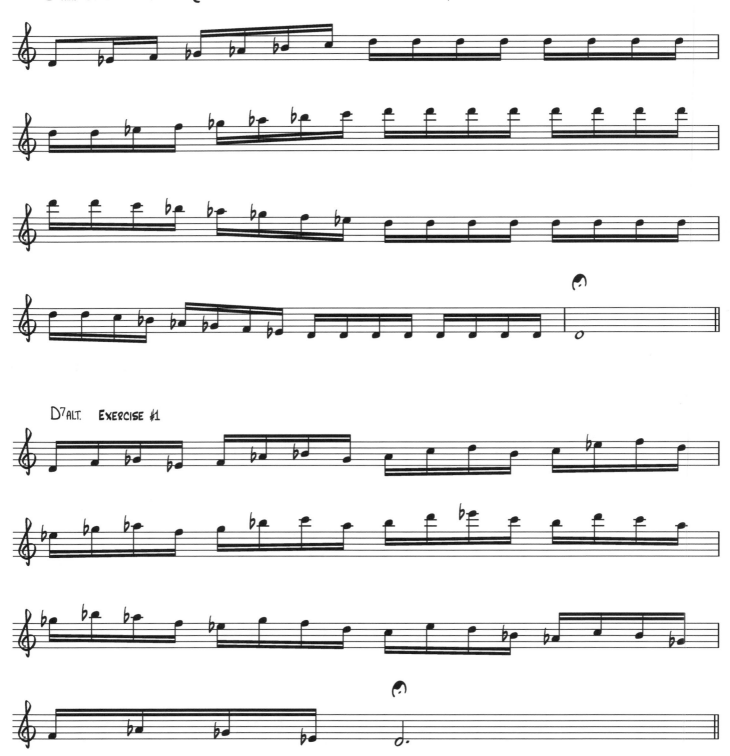

D⁷ALT. EXERCISE #1

D *(continued)*

D⁷ALT. EXERCISE #2

D⁷ALT. EXERCISE #3

D⁷ALT. EXERCISE #4

D⁷ALT. EXERCISE #5

5 Qualities of the 7th Chord

Diatonic 7th Chords—Major

Eb *(continued)*

Diatonic 7th Chords—Melodic Minor

Diatonic 7th Chords—Harmonic Minor

E♭ *(continued)*

Superlocrian—7th Mode, Melodic Minor

E♭7 ALT.   SUPERLOCRIAN SCALE (USE ANY OTHER SCALE YOU'D LIKE TO WORK ON)

E♭7 ALT.   EXERCISE #1

E♭ (continued)

E♭7 ALT. EXERCISE #2

E♭7 ALT. EXERCISE #3

E♭7 ALT. EXERCISE #4

E♭7 ALT. EXERCISE #5

E

5 Qualities of the 7th Chord

Diatonic 7th Chords—Major

E *(continued)*

Diatonic 7th Chords—Melodic Minor

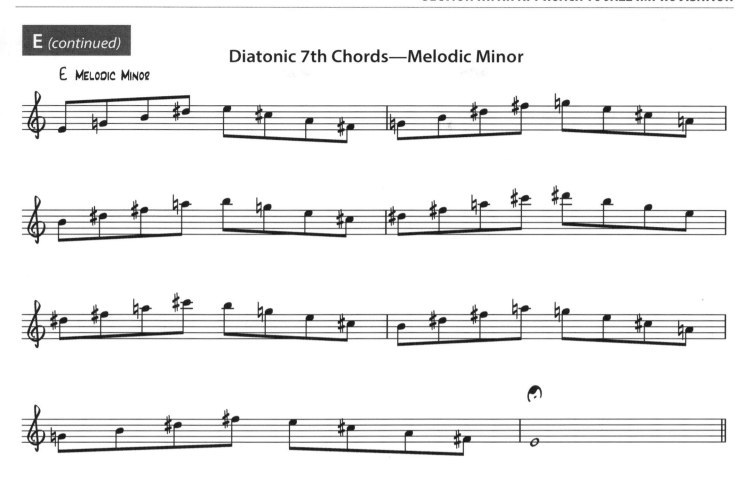

Diatonic 7th Chords—Harmonic Minor

E *(continued)*

Superlocrian—7th Mode, Melodic Minor

E⁷ALT.   SUPERLOCRIAN SCALE (USE ANY OTHER SCALE YOU'D LIKE TO WORK ON)

E⁷ALT.   EXERCISE #1

E *(continued)*

E⁷ᴀʟᴛ. Exercise #2

E⁷ᴀʟᴛ. Exercise #3

E⁷ᴀʟᴛ. Exercise #4

E⁷ᴀʟᴛ. Exercise #5

F

5 Qualities of the 7th Chord

Diatonic 7th Chords—Major

F (continued)

Diatonic 7th Chords—Melodic Minor

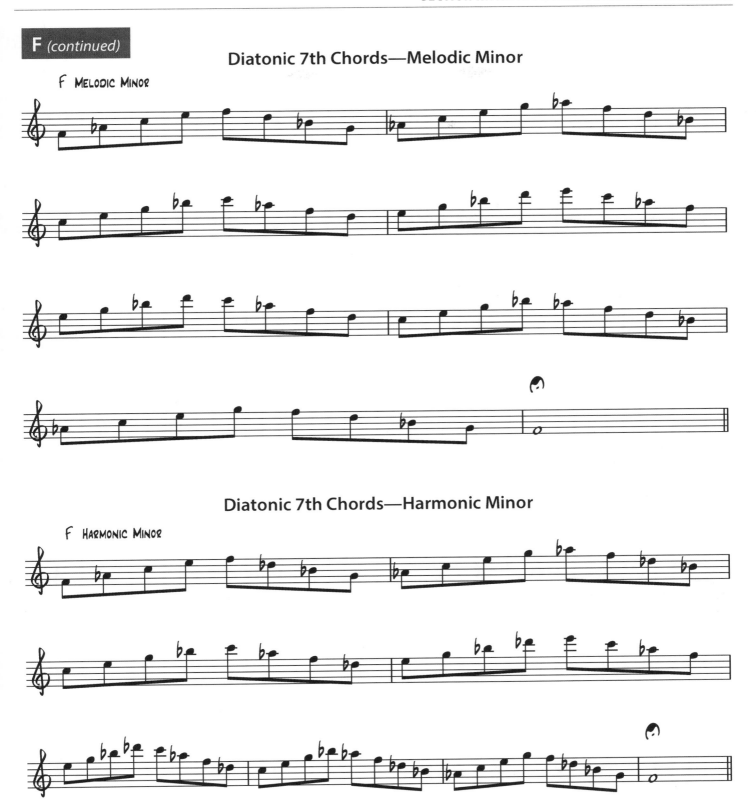

Diatonic 7th Chords—Harmonic Minor

F *(continued)*

Superlocrian—7th Mode, Melodic Minor

F *(continued)*

F⁷ ALT. EXERCISE #2

F⁷ ALT. EXERCISE #3

F⁷ ALT. EXERCISE #4

F⁷ ALT. EXERCISE #5

F# *8va*

5 Qualities of the 7th Chord

Diatonic 7th Chords—Major

F# *8va (continued)*

Diatonic 7th Chords—Melodic Minor

F# MELODIC MINOR

Diatonic 7th Chords—Harmonic Minor

F# HARMONIC MINOR

F# *8va (continued)*

Superlocrian—7th Mode, Melodic Minor

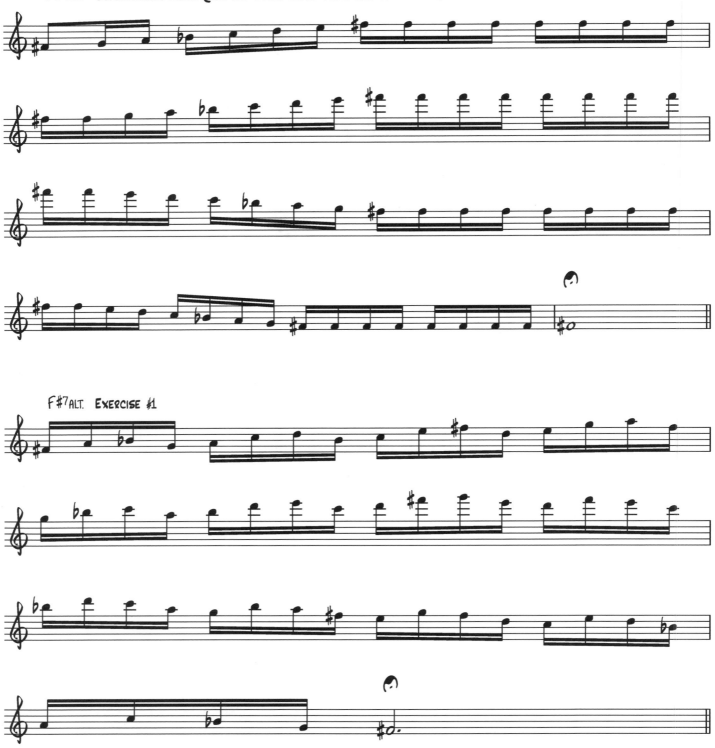

F# *8va (continued)*

F#7 ALT. EXERCISE #2

F#7 ALT. EXERCISE #3

F#7 ALT. EXERCISE #4

F#7 ALT. EXERCISE #5

SECTION IV: JAZZ ETUDES

In Section IV we apply some of the Chordal and Scale Exercises to Chord progressions of Jazz Standards.

You'll mostly find the Super Locrian (or Altered) scale over the altered V7♭9♭13 chord, the Mixolydian over the regular V7 chord, Dorian over the ii chord, 2nd Mode Harmonic Minor over the iimin7♭5 and 5th Mode Harmonic Minor over the V7♭9 Chord.

Those are just some of the options available. Make sure to explore other options for your own Improvisation, for example—a Lydian Dominant over the V chord, which will give you a different color than just the Mixolydian, since it has the #11 in the scale.

Go back to the Major Modes, Melodic Minor Modes & Harmonic Minor Modes in Section III and start matching the Chord Symbols to the related Scales.

Solo Over Blues in G

BY STEFFEN KUEHN

Solo Over Rhythm Changes in C

BY STEFFEN KUEHN

It Was Never About You

BY STEFFEN KUEHN

Friendly People

BY STEFFEN KUEHN

Digame

BY STEFFEN KUEHN

Mostly Your Items

BY STEFFEN KUEHN

Laurels

BY STEFFEN KUEHN

55901080R00048

Made in the USA
Columbia, SC
18 April 2019